MONICA BELLUCCI

A Timeless Journey of Beauty and Talent Through the World of Cinema and Beyond

MATTIE SNOW

Copyright @ 2024 By Mattie Snow

All rights reserved. No part of this book may be reproduced, distributed, or transmitted in any form or by any means, including photocopying, recording, or other electronic or mechanical methods, without the prior written permission of the publisher, except in the case of brief quotations embodied in critical reviews and specific other noncommercial uses permitted by copyright law.

Contents

INTRODUCTION

ITALIAN BEGINNINGS

FROM LAW TO THE RUNWAY

BREAKING INTO FILM

THE GLOBAL STAR

A BOND GIRL AND BEYOND

BEAUTY AND EMPOWERMENT

PERSONAL LIFE AND RELATIONSHIPS

MULTILINGUAL MASTERY

THE ART OF REINVENTION

BEYOND THE SCREEN

LEGACY OF AN ICON

CONCLUSION

INTRODUCTION

Monica Bellucci's name is linked with ageless elegance, yet there is much more to her than meets the eye. She is a woman who has defied not only beauty standards but also the expectations of an industry that sometimes confines women to one-dimensional roles. Monica exemplifies the belief that true power is gained by breaking the mold rather than fitting into it. Her journey from the humble streets of Città di Castello to the world's most glamorous red carpets is more than just a story of fame and money. It's a story of personal discovery, resilience, and uninhibited self-expression that has captivated audiences and lovers worldwide.

Born in 1964, Monica was not raised in a privileged or glamorous environment. Her early life was simple, far from the glamor of the international fashion and entertainment industries that she would one day dominate. Raised in a modest home, she learned the value of hard work and independence at a young age.

These lessons would be necessary in a career that, while frequently recognized, was challenging. Monica was a young woman with dreams long before she graced the covers of Vogue or walked the red carpets of Cannes—and those dreams had nothing to do with being in the spotlight.

Monica's earliest objectives were intellectual. She enrolled in law school to pursue a legal career. It appeared to be a practical path for a young woman with aspirations but had different intentions. Monica began modeling to help pay for her studies, and it wasn't long before fashion professionals noticed her beautiful appearance and compelling presence. What began as a means to an end quickly evolved into the start of an entirely new chapter. Monica's modeling career opened doors she had never anticipated, and while the decision to forgo her legal studies was difficult, it became evident that her future lay elsewhere.

However, unlike many models who transferred into acting, Monica's journey to film prominence was not motivated by superficiality. From the start, she handled her work with depth and intention, looking for parts that allowed her to delve into the depths of human nature. Her first significant film appearances were in Italian cinema, where she immediately established a reputation for conveying fragility and strength. While her beauty opened doors, her talent, emotional intelligence, and unwavering dedication carried her to the pinnacle of the film industry.

Monica's breakthrough role occurred in 2000 with the film *Malèna*, which solidified her status as an international sensation. In *Malèna*, she played a lady whose beauty became both her greatest asset and her most considerable burden—a mirror, perhaps, of the conflicts she faced in her personal life. It was a role that struck a chord with viewers, not just because of Monica's innate beauty but also because of her raw passion and sensitivity to the character. *Malèna* was a watershed event in her career and the point at which the world recognized her as more than just a beautiful face.

Monica's attractiveness stems from her paradoxes. She exudes traditional, old-world glamor while remaining fiercely modern and progressive in her attitude towards life and work. She has never let her appearance define her or followed Hollywood's strict standards. Monica refused to succumb to the constraints of maintaining an appearance of eternal youth as she rose to become one of the world's most recognizable faces. In an industry that frequently discards women above a certain age, she has boldly accepted her age and become an ardent advocate for changing beauty standards.

Her choice of characters demonstrates her depth and reluctance to be stereotyped. Monica has always strived to challenge herself and defy expectations, whether in dramatic parts exploring the human condition's intricacies or high-octane action pictures like *The Matrix Reloaded* and *Spectre*. In *Spectre*, she became the oldest actress ever cast as a Bond woman, breaking the franchise's conventional mold of youth-obsessed casting and sending a striking statement about the ongoing attraction and relevance of women beyond their twenties and thirties. This was more than just a position; it was a message.

While her filmography is tremendous, Monica's influence extends beyond the screen. She has always been fiercely guarded, especially in her personal life, which includes a high-profile marriage to actor Vincent Cassel, with whom she has two daughters. Despite their final split, Monica has remained a loving mother, carefully balancing her professional obligations with her domestic commitments. Monica's family is her anchor, and she has always stated that her roles as a mother and woman are just as essential, if not more so, than her professional accomplishments.

Monica is well-known off-screen for her humanitarian activities, particularly her support for women's rights and involvement in various charitable organizations. She has utilized her platform to advocate for topics ranging from gender equality to the representation of women in the media, always with the grace and intelligence that have distinguished her career. In a business where many actors lose relevance as they age, Monica has demonstrated that reinvention is possible at any stage of life. She has constantly grown, refusing to be limited by the usual expectations imposed on women in Hollywood.

As we explore Monica Bellucci's life and career, we'll discover a story beyond the standard Hollywood narrative. Her story is more than beauty or celebrity; it's about strength, determination, and sincerity. Monica has always lived life on her terms, rejecting the constraints of an industry obsessed with youth and perfection, from her early years in Italy to her current status as a global movie star. Her story celebrates what it means to be a woman, a mother, an artist, and, most importantly, a human being—flawed, complex, and infinitely intriguing.

In this biography, we'll look at Monica's life in all facets:
The teenager who aspired to be a lawyer.
The model who became a muse.
The actress who redefined what it meant to be a leading lady.

The mother who always stayed grounded.

One thing that has remained constant throughout is Monica's unshakeable devotion to being herself. She is and will always be more than just a symbol of beauty. She is a lady of substance, power, and grace, and her journey is inspiring and unusual. This is Monica Bellucci's story—one of reinvention, endurance, and the timeless elegance of being unapologetic about oneself.

Chapter 1

ITALIAN BEGINNINGS

Monica Bellucci's narrative begins in the tranquil and lovely village of Città di Castello, in the heart of Umbria, Italy. Monica was born on September 30, 1964, and grew up in a simple and traditional setting. While lacking the flash and glamor for which she would later be known, her youth laid the groundwork for the grounded and tough woman she would become. Città di Castello, surrounded by rolling hills and historically rich terrain, gave a peaceful setting that nurtured a strong appreciation for family, culture, and hard work.

Monica was the only child of Brunella, an avid amateur painter, and Pasquale, the proprietor of a small trucking company. Monica's parents, despite leading regular lives, played an exceptional impact in forming her viewpoint. Her father taught her the value of discipline and perseverance. Pasquale was a hard worker who cared profoundly for his family. Though his life was not luxurious, he personified the principles of responsibility and integrity, teaching his daughter that success in any area is won through hard work and determination.

Monica inherited her mother's love of creativity and the arts. Though Brunella was not a professional artist, her love of painting instilled in their family an appreciation for beauty in all its manifestations. Monica would frequently watch her mother produce art, noticing the delicate but strong strokes of the brush and understanding that art could say what words couldn't. Monica's early exposure to artistic expression informed her sensibilities, igniting a passion for cinema, fashion, and storytelling that would later characterize her career. Her mother's loving presence contrasted with her father's hard-working personality, teaching her that beauty, whether in art or life, should be valued but not the exclusive measure of worth.

The rhythms of small-town Italy shaped Monica's childhood in Città di Castello. Far from the chaos of modern urban life, the village had a peaceful charm, with the local people taking center stage. Monica attended local schools and was known as an intelligent but reclusive young lady. She was a hard-working student who excelled in class and was naturally interested in life outside her tiny community. Despite her shyness, Monica retained an inner power that would eventually become a defining feature of her personality. She did not desire attention or pursue the glamour her beauty would inevitably bring her. Instead, her early objectives were academic, with her first desire of becoming a lawyer.

In fact, before becoming an international superstar, Monica was on track to practice law in the Italian legal system. After finishing her education at Città di Castello, she enrolled at the University of Perugia, a prestigious university in the area. Her decision to study law was motivated by her intellect and ambition to pursue a career based on content rather than appearance. For a while, she appeared destined to become a lawyer, working hard to reconcile her studies with a growing interest in other prospects that had emerged.

Monica's beauty became more noticeable as she grew older. She was tall, had dark hair, gorgeous Mediterranean features, and a solid yet graceful presence. People in her community and beyond began to take notice of her unique appearance. Local photographers and modeling companies in Italy started approaching her with model offers. Monica was initially reluctant. She wanted to continue her legal education and enter an industry that she believed would primarily focus on her physical attractiveness. However, the offers continued, and she eventually agreed to do some modeling work to help pay for her tuition.

What began as a means to an end quickly evolved into the start of something far more significant. Monica's inherent grace and unmistakable beauty drew the attention of fashion professionals well beyond her modest Italian town. As she matched her law studies with modeling jobs, it became evident that she could excel globally. Monica's first steps into the fashion industry were tentative. Still, as she gained experience, she realized that modeling offered her more than simply financial stability—it provided a platform for expression and creativity.

Her long-term aspirations did not include working in the fashion sector. Despite her burgeoning modeling fame, Monica stayed committed to her schooling. She continued her legal studies, determined to complete what she had begun. But the responsibilities of her burgeoning modeling career began to tug her in a new direction. The turning point occurred when she was offered to relocate to Milan, Italy's fashion capital, and pursue modeling full-time. It was a difficult decision—on the one hand, she had spent years studying law; on the other, the modeling industry allowed her to broaden her horizons.

Monica eventually decided to take a leap of faith. She relocated to Milan, completely immersing herself in high fashion. It was a difficult decision, but one that would be transformational. Modeling introduced her to some of the world's most renowned designers and photographers, and her face soon appeared on the covers of top fashion magazines. Despite her success, Monica never forgot her beginnings. She stayed rooted in the principles taught to her by her parents and upbringing in Città di Castello—humility, the value of hard effort, and the understanding that true beauty goes well beyond physical appearance.

Monica's early existence in Italy was more than simply a backdrop to her achievement; it was an essential component of who she would become. The peaceful streets, the rolling hills, and her mother's artistic energy helped shape her identity. Monica brought the essence of her Italian roots with her as she traveled from small-town Italy to the world stage—a profound connection to family, an unbreakable work ethic, and a belief that true success is measured not by celebrity but by one's ability to remain honest and grounded in the midst of it.

Thus, Monica Bellucci's Italian upbringing provides insight into the formative years of a lady who would go on to capture the world with her beauty and strength, intelligence, and grace. Her journey from the small town of Città di Castello to the pinnacle of international success exemplifies the enduring power of roots and how they influence a career and a whole life.

Chapter 2

FROM LAW TO THE RUNWAY

Monica Bellucci was at a crossroads in her life in the late 1980s, and the world awaited her decision—a decision that would forever change her destiny. With her law studies at the University of Perugia in full swing, she imagined a career dedicated to justice, where she could use her brain to establish a name for herself in the legal sector. However, the enticing appeal of the fashion world, which was bright and brimming with innovation, drew her in. It was a world where beauty and artistry collided, and despite her initial doubts, Monica became enthralled by the prospect of a life in front of the camera rather than behind a judicial desk.

Monica's modeling career began somewhat suddenly. Initially, she took on modeling gigs to help pay for her tuition, seeing them as a transient solution rather than a long-term investment. With her beautiful features—dark, expressive eyes and flowing raven hair—she was rapidly discovered by local photographers and modeling agencies, and what began as a source of income quickly became a thriving business. Despite her success in the design industry, Monica stayed committed to her academic goals, pursuing a law degree.

However, as modeling chances increased, Monica was presented with a dilemma: the more successful she grew in fashion, the more appealing it looked to forsake her legal studies completely. The turning point came with an opportunity to relocate to Milan, Italy's fashion capital. With its sparkling runways and renowned designers, the city promised an exciting life of opportunities and status. After careful contemplation, Monica bravely decided to prioritize her modeling career, abandoning the legal path she had methodically mapped out. It was a leap of trust that would quickly prove revolutionary.

Monica was captivated by Milan's hectic energy from the moment she arrived. Every area brimmed with imagination, and she instantly embraced her new surroundings. Her initial modeling assignments began to pile up, with prominent fashion brands taking notice of her alluring appearance. She walked the runways for top designers such as Dolce & Gabbana, Versace, and Roberto Cavalli, quickly establishing herself as an industry icon. The exhilaration of the runway, with its dazzling lights and screaming acclaim, was addictive, and Monica flourished in the spotlight.

Despite the grandeur surrounding her, switching to a full-time modeling job was not easy. The fashion industry can be rigorous and unforgiving, necessitating perseverance and a firm dedication to one's art. Monica faced the challenge of maintaining her image while navigating the nuances of the company. However, the solid foundation of her upbringing in Città di Castello allowed her to face the pressures of fame. Her parents had instilled in her the principles of hard labor, tenacity, and humility—characteristics that would serve her well as she navigated the volatile fashion world.

Monica's popularity was built not just on her striking appearance but also on her ability to connect with viewers. Each photo shoot and runway show allowed her to convey a story and elicit emotion. Unlike many models who depended exclusively on their appearance, Monica gave her work depth and personality, embodying the roles she represented. This intrinsic talent was not lost on photographers and directors, who saw her as a force to be reckoned with, capable of conveying more than just the most recent trends.

Opportunities in the film industry grew in tandem with her modeling career. It wasn't long before filmmakers approached her, drawn by her fascinating presence and compelling charisma. Her film debut came in 1990 with the Italian film "La Riffa," when she exhibited both her acting and modeling abilities. Monica's transition from runway to screen was effortless; her modeling background had prepared her to perform gracefully and confidently in front of the camera. She immediately became a skilled actor, seamlessly transitioning between genres and captivated audiences with her performances.

Monica's journey from the law to the runway demonstrated her capacity to embrace change and adapt to new difficulties. The world of fashion provided her with not only prominence but also a forum to express herself creatively. She symbolizes empowerment, demonstrating that women could achieve in various fields, combining beauty with intelligence and creativity. Her story touched many people, encouraging aspiring models and actresses who viewed her as a reflection of their goals.

Despite the glitz and splendor, Monica remained true to her Italian roots. She frequently pondered on her background in Città di Castello, appreciating the ideals instilled in her by her parents. They had taught her the value of authenticity and keeping true to oneself, which helped her negotiate the complications of celebrity and success. Despite the swirl of events around her, Monica always made time for family and friends, keeping her life in balance with the stress of her job.

Monica Bellucci became a cultural phenomenon and a fashion icon throughout time. Her rare blend of beauty, talent, and charisma captivated audiences worldwide. She appeared on innumerable magazine covers as a muse for well-known designers and rose to become one of the highest-paid models of her time. However, her triumph was not achieved without personal sacrifices. The industry's demands frequently required long hours and substantial travel, which tested her tenacity and dedication to her art.

Monica began to take on more challenging film parts as her artistic development progressed. Her performances in international blockbusters such as "The Matrix Reloaded" and "The Passion of the Christ" demonstrated her versatility and ability to portray various personalities. Critics praised her for her depth and emotional range, cementing her reputation as a superb actress. Her career path, from law to the runway and eventually to

Hollywood, demonstrated the importance of following one's passion and accepting the unknown.

Monica Bellucci's journey from ambitious lawyer to successful model and actress provides an uplifting story of self-discovery and courage. It emphasizes the significance of keeping open to life's opportunities, even if they differ from the plans we make for ourselves. Monica's decision to pursue her passion for modeling revolutionized her life. It encouraged numerous others to take risks and follow their ambitions, demonstrating that often, the most rewarding roads are those we never intended to take.

Chapter 3

BREAKING INTO FILM

As Monica Bellucci negotiated the thrilling world of modeling in the 1990s, her remarkable presence and charisma quickly drew the attention of filmmakers eager to capitalize on her distinctive appeal. While she had established herself as a top model, walking the runways of Milan and appearing in high-profile commercial campaigns, the pull of acting beckoned to her—a realm where she could explore the depths of her creativity and demonstrate her talents outside of fashion. This leap from the runway to the big screen was more than just a professional change; it was a calling that would alter her artistic identity and solidify her status as a multidimensional performer.

Monica's acting career began with her role in the 1990 Italian film "La Riffa," a love drama that introduced her to the film business and showed her promise as an actress. In this film, she played a beautiful woman caught up in a love triangle, demonstrating her ability to inspire strong emotions and represent complex characters. Although her performance received only minor praise, it paved the way for future opportunities and marked the start of a new chapter in her life. She approached acting with the same zeal she had devoted to her modeling career, knowing that she would need to develop her craft to thrive in this competitive industry.

Monica soon rose to prominence in the Italian cinema industry, landing roles in various projects that allowed her to experiment with diverse genres. In 1992, she appeared in "Bram Stoker's Dracula", directed by Francis Ford Coppola, as the vampire's alluring wife. This multinational effort was a watershed moment in her career, introducing her to a larger audience and cementing her reputation as a forceful presence in Hollywood. Working with famous filmmakers and actresses gave her the necessary knowledge and insight into the acting craft, allowing her to fine-tune her skills while broadening her horizons.

Monica's path continued with her role in the film "Malèna" (2000), directed by Giuseppe Tornatore. She played the title character in this moving coming-of-age narrative set in Sicily during World War II, a beautiful lady who becomes the object of longing and scorn in her little town. Monica's exceptional ability to communicate sensitivity and strength simultaneously was fully displayed throughout the picture, capturing both spectators and critics. Her portrayal earned her several honors, including nominations for significant awards, cementing her place as one of Italy's top actors.

Despite her growing fame, Monica faced the hurdles of transitioning from model to actress in a film business that is generally skeptical of such changes. Critics and audiences sometimes failed to look past her modeling background, and she had to show her acting ability again. However, she faced these hurdles with tenacity, determined to show that her brilliance stretched far beyond her appearance. She immersed herself in her parts, thoroughly studying them and performing authentically.

Monica's film career grew as she collaborated with renowned directors and worked on numerous projects across genres. Her performance as Persephone in the 2003 film "The Matrix Reloaded" propelled her to a global audience, allowing her to perform alongside famous Hollywood stars such as Keanu Reeves and Laurence Fishburne. This experience advanced her career and demonstrated her ability to thrive in high-pressure situations and compete with industry heavyweights.

Monica's drive to excel as an actor prompted her to pursue international roles, extending her appeal. She appeared in films such as "Irreversible" (2002), a controversial French thriller directed by Gaspar Noé, in which she played a woman imprisoned in a devastating cycle of violence. This part pushed the limits of her acting ability, allowing her to explore darker subjects and demonstrate her versatility as a performer. Despite the film's complex subject matter, Monica's performance received critical acclaim and displayed her willingness to take risks in pursuing her profession.

Monica Bellucci always sought jobs that pushed her and allowed her to grow throughout her career in film. She preferred complex characters, frequently presenting women dealing with their desires, challenges, and inner conflicts. This depth of characterization struck a chord with spectators, cementing her reputation as an actor capable of generating powerful emotions and connecting with them.

Monica's captivating charisma continued to draw the attention of the fashion world, and she managed to juggle her two occupations smoothly. She remained a popular model while aggressively pursuing acting opportunities, seamlessly shifting between the two worlds. Her ability to transition across industries demonstrated her adaptability and dedication to her craft, allowing her to preserve her image as a fashion star while still establishing herself as a professional actress.

Chapter 4

THE GLOBAL STAR

Few cinema performances capture the sheer intensity of vulnerability and beauty, like Monica Bellucci's portrayal of Malèna Scordia in Giuseppe Tornatore's film *Malèna* (2000). The film, set in Sicily during World War II, follows the story of Renato, a young lad whose fascination with the lovely Malèna changes his life forever. This film marked a watershed moment in Monica's career and cemented her status as a global icon, eternally linking her legacy to her iconic character.

Monica Bellucci, born in Città di Castello, Italy, was already a well-known model before pursuing a career in acting. However, *Malèna* was the film that demonstrated her outstanding talent and ability to inhabit a character. The film's plot is told from the perspective of Renato, who falls in love with Malèna, a lady who represents both beauty and sorrow. As the play progresses, the spectator sees the societal consequences of her allure: the town's men covet her, while the women harbor jealousy and scorn, transforming Malèna into a symbol of desire and hatred.

Bellucci's portrayal in *Malèna* demonstrates her ability to convey complicated emotions, conveying the essence of a woman whose beauty empowers her and makes her vulnerable. She delicately handles the character's journey, allowing viewers to sense her anguish and isolation amidst the societal instability around her. The richness of her portrayal elicits intense empathy, converting Malèna from a mere object of desire into a multidimensional woman whose sufferings are shared by anybody who has endured judgment and ostracism.

Upon its premiere, *Malèna* received widespread acclaim and was screened at the Cannes Film Festival, where it became an instant classic. Critics praised Bellucci's compelling performance, emphasizing how she imbued Malèna with strength and vulnerability. Her performance earned her numerous accolades and prizes, cementing her status as one of Italy's finest actors and paving the road for her worldwide career. The film became a cultural phenomenon, resonating with viewers worldwide and cementing Monica's image as a rising star.

Monica Bellucci's success with *Malèna* offered her new opportunities, allowing her to play various roles and work with renowned filmmakers. Following her debut performance, she moved smoothly into foreign movies. One of her significant later films was *Irreversible* (2002), a daring French thriller directed by Gaspar Noé, in which she delivered an outstanding performance that demonstrated her ability to confront complex and contentious subjects. The film's raw intensity and unsettling plot cemented her image as a bold actor prepared to push the limits of storytelling.

Bellucci has shown her versatility and ability to flourish in high-stakes, blockbuster situations by sharing the screen with A-list performers such as Keanu Reeves and Laurence Fishburne. Her appearance in these films attracted a larger audience and secured her reputation as a notable personality in Hollywood. The character Persephone, a woman imprisoned between worlds, reflects Monica's career as an Italian actress and international fame.

Monica's success extended beyond her film appearances; she became a fashion star, appearing on the covers of major publications and walking the runways of famous fashion firms. Her distinctive combination of beauty, elegance, and talent made her a popular figure in fashion and cinema. Despite her growing celebrity, she stayed grounded, frequently reflecting on her Italian origins and the impact of her childhood on her art. Monica's honesty struck a chord with fans and filmmakers alike, gaining her respect and appreciation in an industry that frequently prioritizes superficiality.

Throughout her career, Monica Bellucci chose roles that pushed her and allowed her to explore challenging subjects. In Mel Gibson's 2004 film *The Passion of the Christ*, she played Mary Magdalene, a part that required emotional depth and spiritual resonance. The film's outstanding storytelling and Monica's moving performance cemented her reputation as an actress capable of communicating tremendous emotion and complexity.

Monica Bellucci broke Hollywood's traditional aging norms as she entered her forties and beyond. She embraced roles that matched her maturity and experience, demonstrating that women can continue to play intriguing characters at any age. Her performances in films like *Spectre* (2015) showed her ability to play forceful and appealing characters, breaking industry stereotypes of female leads. As a result, she became an advocate for women in film, promoting more diverse and realistic portrayals of women on screen.

Monica's rise to global popularity is marked by her outstanding performances and resilience in the face of a rapidly changing film industry. She frequently emphasized the value of remaining true to oneself and pursuing one's passions without compromise. Her tale inspires aspiring actors and actresses worldwide, reminding them that success is possible with hard work, authenticity, and a desire to accept vulnerability and strength.

Chapter 5

A BOND GIRL AND BEYOND

Monica Bellucci's performance of Lucia Sciarra in *Spectre* (2015) was a watershed moment in her career and the representation of female characters in the James Bond franchise. Her casting as the oldest Bond girl at 50 was daring, breaking customary expectations in a profession frequently obsessed with youth. In a critical scene, she gave an enthralling performance that showed fragility and strength, surpassing the superficiality associated with the Bond girl stereotype. Lucia is defined not only by her relationship with James Bond but also by her narrative arc, which makes her central to the film's plot. This richness provided audiences with a character they could relate to, reflecting the complex reality of women's lives rather than mere fiction.

Bellucci's relationship with Daniel Craig, who played Lucia Sciarra, demonstrated her ability to bring the character to life. Their exchanges were filled with seriousness, transforming what could have been a one-dimensional part into a rich tapestry of emotional undercurrents. The film explored themes of loss, fidelity, and the cost of love, and Bellucci's acting was crucial in communicating these ideas. Critics commended her for adding depth and complexity to the film, portraying a woman who, despite her flaws, wielded her power in a dangerous world.

Monica Bellucci's shift to *Spectre* was not an isolated occasion; it was the product of years of carefully chosen parts that demonstrated her versatility as an actress. Following her successful modeling career, she smoothly transitioned into acting, taking on various parts that showed her depth and versatility. Her flexibility was evident in her early career in Italian cinema when she worked in films such as *Malèna* (2000). In that film, she played a young widow in a Sicilian village, impressing spectators with a performance that addressed themes of desire, solitude, and society's harsh judgments. Her portrayal of Malèna was more than just a beauty story; it was an investigation of the human condition, capturing the hardships of a woman who became both an object of want and a source of jealousy.

Following her triumph in Italian cinema, Bellucci established herself worldwide with films like *The Matrix Reloaded* (2003) and *The Matrix Revolutions* (2003), in which she played the intriguing figure Persephone. In this part, she demonstrated her ability to traverse complex stories while maintaining mystery and intrigue. The Matrix trilogy allowed her to venture into the world of science fiction, showing her versatility as an actress who can handle various genres, from drama to action.

Bellucci's position as a Bond girl in *Spectre* was more than just a continuation of her film career; it was a reinvention of the character itself. Unlike previous generations of Bond ladies, whose stories frequently revolved around seduction and danger, Lucia Sciarra was a character with agency and depth. Bellucci's performance portrayed a lady who had been through love, sorrow, and betrayal, making her sympathetic to modern audiences. The film's plot implies that while James Bond symbolizes strength and charisma, Lucia is also influential in her own right. Her decisions and sacrifices defined her life, and her relationship with Bond evolved into mutual respect rather than sheer desire.

Monica Bellucci continued to push herself as an actress in the years following *Spectre*, taking on different roles that demonstrated her versatility. In *The Brothers Bloom* (2008), she portrayed the charismatic Penelope Stamp, who is seduced into the complex plans of two con artists brothers. Her performance struck a balance between charm and wit, allowing fans to glimpse a lighter, more fun side of Bellucci while still communicating emotional depth. Her ability to transition between genres, from romantic dramas to whimsical comedies, illustrates her diverse talent and reluctance to be typecast.

Another vital production in her post-bond career was *On the Milky Road* (2016), directed by Emir Kusturica. Bellucci played a lady caught up in wartime turbulence, with themes of love and conflict intertwined. Her performance was heartbreaking and expressive, showcasing a woman's fortitude in the face of disaster. This picture allowed Bellucci to dig into the depths of love and survival, cementing her reputation as an actress who is not hesitant to take on complex subjects.

Bellucci's contributions to cinema go beyond her performances. She has become a symbol of empowerment, breaking industry standards for age and attractiveness. Her career is an example to actresses everywhere, demonstrating skill and devotion are not limited by age. Bellucci has stated in interviews that she believes women are typically undervalued in the film industry and has committed her career to showing differently. She advocates for a more diverse representation of women on screen by playing parts highlighting the breadth of female perspectives.

Monica Bellucci has evolved in recent years, taking on roles that reflect her professional development as an actress. In *The Matrix Resurrections* (2021), she returned to the renowned franchise as Persephone. This comeback was more than just a nostalgic reference to her previous work; it also provided an opportunity to examine her character's maturation inside a fresh plot. The film's success confirmed Bellucci's place in cinematic history and her ability to grapple with contemporary concerns while remaining true to the franchise's roots.

Monica Bellucci continues to be a formidable force in the film business as she embarks on new chapters in her career. Her performance in *Spectre* and subsequent films cemented her reputation as a versatile actress capable of defying genres and preconceptions. With each performance, she challenges the narrative around women in cinema, demonstrating that a woman's worth is determined not by her age or appearance but by the richness of her character and the depth of her tale.

Monica Bellucci stands out in the ever-changing cinematic scene as a beacon of empowerment, inspiring future generations to accept their uniqueness and pursue their ambitions, no matter what barriers arise. Her transformation from Bond girl to varied actor demonstrates her remarkable talent and determination to reimagine what it means to be a woman in the film industry.

Chapter 6

BEAUTY AND EMPOWERMENT

Monica Bellucci has long been admired not only for her beautiful beauty but also for her profound understanding of womanhood and empowerment. As a lady who has adorned the covers of numerous fashion magazines and acted in significant films worldwide, she has frequently been at the center of arguments about beauty standards, particularly those related to aging. Monica has long believed that true beauty is more than just youth or physical looks; instead, she sees it as a manifestation of confidence, experience, and sincerity.

Bellucci has regularly aired her opinions on society's unreasonable beauty standards for women. In interviews, she stated that the industry frequently promotes a narrow concept of beauty that prioritizes youth above wisdom and experience. For Monica, beauty is more than physical characteristics; it also includes a woman's power, tenacity, and the stories she carries with her. She promotes the idea that women should embrace their originality and enjoy their distinctive traits, acknowledging that beauty may take many forms, often becoming more prosperous and complicated with age.

Her outlook on aging is incredibly refreshing in an industry that sometimes glorifies youth to older women's detriment. Monica famously said, "I believe that beauty is a state of mind." If you are unafraid of aging, you will be more beautiful." This ideology expresses her belief that aging is a natural aspect of life that may be viewed favorably. She urges women to accept the changes that come with aging, viewing them as opportunities for growth and self-discovery rather than losses to mourn.

Monica's experience in modeling and acting has given her a platform to promote these principles. She recognizes the value of representation and visibility for women of all ages. She challenges the clichés about aging in the entertainment industry by continuing to play various roles as she gets older. Her appearance on TV serves as a reminder that women may be strong and beautiful at any age.

Monica has frequently played characters who are strong and independent throughout her career. From the impassioned Malèna to the intriguing Persephone in *The Matrix*, she has constantly portrayed women who are nuanced, multidimensional, and unashamedly themselves. By describing such individuals, she offers a strong message to her audience: women should not be defined exclusively by their relationships or physical appearances but also by their choices, desires, and the richness of their inner lives.

Furthermore, Bellucci's prominence as a female empowerment figure extends beyond her movie performances. She has frequently expressed her belief in the value of sisterhood and female solidarity. In her interviews, she emphasizes women's need to support one another and tear barriers caused by competitiveness or jealousy. Monica believes true empowerment comes from bringing others up and appreciating their triumphs rather than perceiving them as threats. This sense of community is critical for creating an environment where women feel comfortable expressing their identities.

Monica has also tackled the self-acceptance problem and the pressures women endure to meet cultural standards. In a world where women are continually bombarded with messages about how they should look, behave, and age, she advocates for a shift in mindset that prioritizes self-care and acceptance. Bellucci frequently recounts her personal experiences in overcoming fears and achieving inner serenity. She believes beauty is a personal journey, not a competition, and women should value their bodies and experiences.

Monica lives by this idea. She has been open about her difficulties, including balancing the intricacies of being a public figure, mother, and professional. Her ability to juggle these positions while remaining true resonates with many women seeking to find their way in a society that frequently expects perfection. By sharing her story, she creates a sense of relatability, inspiring people to face themselves confidently and gracefully.

Monica Bellucci, an actress who has collaborated with some of the world's most renowned directors and actresses, recognizes the importance of representation in film and media. She continues to advocate for a diverse narrative reflecting the realities of women's lives, urging the industry to broaden its scope. Her efforts aim to promote storylines that showcase women's strength and complexity, enabling a broader view of what it means to be feminine.

Chapter 7

PERSONAL LIFE AND RELATIONSHIPS

Monica Bellucci's life is a riveting story of love, parenting, and the complications of being in the public eye. Monica was born in Città di Castello, Italy, in 1964 and grew up in a loving household that instilled in her strong values and a deep appreciation for relationships. From a young age, she realized the value of connection, loyalty and the enormous impact that love can have on one's life. These early lessons would influence her relationships as she became one of her generation's most recognized actresses.

Monica's most notable romance was with French actor Vincent Cassel. Their tale began in the late 1990s, when they first met while filming *The Apartment* (1996). Their chemistry instantly sparked a passionate romance that captivated the public's interest. As they handled the obstacles of celebrity together, they established themselves as a power couple, recognized not only for their talent but also for their remarkable good looks and charisma. Their wedding in 1999 was a celebration of their intimate bond, characterized by mutual admiration and respect for one other's work. Monica frequently spoke fondly of their union, praising Vincent as a source of inspiration.

Motherhood has been a tremendously gratifying component of Monica's life, providing joy and purpose beyond her job. In interviews, she discussed how becoming a mother changed her outlook on life, emphasizing the value of loving and guiding her children as they grow. Monica is committed to imparting her kids the qualities she holds dear, like self-confidence, independence, and the courage to pursue their aspirations. She frequently emphasizes the need to provide a nurturing environment for her children to express themselves and discover their personalities without fear of being judged.

Despite their close affinity, Monica and Vincent's marriage was not without difficulties. The pressures of their high-profile occupations and the media's constant attention frequently strained their relationship. They could retain a supportive relationship, often cooperating on creative projects and valuing each other's artistic endeavors. However, in 2013, they announced their split, surprising fans and followers. Monica subsequently stated that their breakup was amicable, emphasizing the necessity of co-parenting and prioritizing their children's well-being. She noted that their love for each other had not faded but evolved into a different type of relationship based on friendship and shared parental obligations.

Monica's experience with dating and relationships became a hot topic after her divorce. While she has been associated with several people in the entertainment world, she has chosen to keep most of her dating life private. This decision illustrates her appreciation of the importance of boundaries and her wish to shield her children from the public limelight. Monica's perspective on love has evolved, prompting her to prioritize real friendships that improve her life over seeking validation through public relationships.

Monica has spoken openly about her difficulties in managing her work and parenting. The film career frequently requires substantial travel and long hours; therefore, she must prioritize spending quality time with her girls. She has openly discussed her problems with finding balance, emphasizing the value of being there in her children's lives despite the responsibilities of her job. Monica has mentioned how she finds delight in ordinary family events, such as cooking together, participating in outdoor activities, or celebrating milestones. These everyday encounters, she says, are what genuinely enhance her life and allow her to keep a close relationship with her girls.

Monica's Italian upbringing has greatly influenced her understanding of love and relationships. She grew up in a family-oriented culture and values loyalty, respect, and friendships formed through shared experiences. Monica frequently focuses on her upbringing, gaining inspiration from the deep bonds she witnessed in her family. This cultural perspective guides her approach to her personal and professional life as she strives to establish genuine connections with those around her.

Monica began a quest of self-discovery following her separation from Cassel. She embraced this phase of her life as an opportunity for personal development, focussing on knowing her identity outside of the responsibilities of wife and mother. Monica has emphasized the importance of self-love and acceptance, acknowledging that a strong sense of self is critical to her happiness and well-being. This journey of empowerment is significant to her admirers because she displays how navigating life's transitions can lead to personal fulfillment and a renewed sense of purpose.

Monica's public appearances and interviews continue to convey a feeling of power and resilience. Her ability to openly discuss her difficulties has made her a role model for many women facing similar challenges. She emphasizes that love and relationships are not always ideal; they necessitate work, understanding, and flexibility. Monica's story motivates others to embrace their experiences, learn from them, and prioritize what truly counts: meaningful connections and love for those who matter most.

Ultimately, Monica Bellucci's personal life and relationships depict a lady who exudes grace, courage, and genuineness. Her path through love, parenting, and self-discovery exemplifies the complications of navigating a high-profile career while remaining true to her ideals. Her marriage to Vincent Cassel and her enduring loyalty to her daughters demonstrate the exquisite interplay of personal fulfillment and familial affection. Monica continues to change, but she remains a beacon of inspiration, urging women everywhere to accept their uniqueness, face life's problems bravely, and love the connections that enrich their lives.

Chapter 8

MULTILINGUAL MASTERY

Monica Bellucci's language prowess is more than just a reflection of her talent; it demonstrates her commitment to her art and deep appreciation for different civilizations. Monica was born in the scenic town of Città di Castello, Italy, and grew up in an arts and communication-focused atmosphere. Her early exposure to numerous languages and cultures paved the way for her future career in film, where her ability to portray emotion and nuance across multiple languages would become one of her most defining characteristics.

Monica had a strong interest in languages since she was very young. She attended high school in her hometown, where she studied English and French, obtaining skills that would be useful in her acting career. Her early motivation to learn languages stemmed from a desire to understand the world outside her small Italian town. She recognized that language is a powerful weapon that allows communication, enriches cultural interchange, and broadens one's perspective.

Monica's linguistic skills proved beneficial as she transitioned from modeling to acting. Her ability to fluently speak Italian, French, and English led to various roles in international cinema, allowing her to collaborate with renowned directors and performers from many countries. She rose to prominence in the Italian cinema, appearing in critically praised films like *Malèna* and *The Brothers Grimm*. However, her ambitions went beyond Italy, as she aimed to establish herself as a versatile actress capable of mesmerizing audiences worldwide.

Monica made her breakthrough in French cinema with her performance in Gaspar Noé's film *Irreversible* (2002). This daring and demanding picture stretched the boundaries and demonstrated her fearless approach to acting. The controversial film gained critical acclaim, cementing her reputation as an actress capable of playing complicated and demanding parts. Her ability to produce a compelling French performance drew notice while demonstrating her dedication to mastering the language. This part constituted a watershed moment in her career, opening the door to new prospects in French cinema.

Monica's venture into English-language films increased her repertory and demonstrated her bilingual expertise. Her performance as a Bond girl in *Spectre* (2015) marked a watershed event in her career, allowing her to connect with a global audience. Monica proved she could hold her own in a blockbuster picture while flawlessly moving between languages by working with legendary actors like Daniel Craig and Léa Seydoux. Her portrayal of Lucia Sciarra was captivating and compelling, capturing the essence of a character who struck a chord with worldwide audiences.

Monica's linguistic ability improved her performance and her interactions with a wide range of collaborators. While working on international projects, she frequently communicated with directors, performers, and crew members in their original languages, which fostered a sense of community and respect. This linguistic flexibility enabled her to immerse herself in each production's local intricacies, resulting in authentic and approachable performances. In films such as *The Passion of the Christ* (2004), where she spoke Aramaic, she faced the task of memorizing lines and genuinely understanding the context and emotional weight of the speech. This commitment to sincerity is a defining feature of her career, allowing her to offer a distinct dimension to each part.

Monica has consistently emphasized the value of language in narrative. She believes learning other languages allows her to embody individuals better and explore their motivations, feelings, and origins. This awareness has encouraged her to pursue jobs that appeal to her, regardless of the language in which they are spoken. She is more than just an actress; she is a storyteller who utilizes language to connect with people on a deeper level. In *The Brothers Bloom* (2008), for example, she expertly handled the complexities of her character's dialogue, demonstrating her ability to adapt to diverse linguistic approaches while preserving the core of her performances.

Monica's experience with language has also shaped her outlook on the film industry. She has frequently discussed the significance of authenticity in cinema, calling for stories that reflect the breadth of the human experience. She advocates for more representation in cinema by deliberately seeking out projects that allow her to interact with people from many cultures and languages. Her performance in *The Man Who Knew Too Much* (2005) demonstrated this dedication, as she immersed herself in the culture and language of the film's location, delivering a level of authenticity that struck a chord with spectators.

In addition to her film work, Monica has used possibilities to promote cultural understanding through her linguistic ability. She has attended foreign film festivals and events, frequently discussing the role of cinema in promoting cross-cultural dialogue. By sharing her experiences and ideas, she promotes the value of various tales in film and the power of language to bridge cultural boundaries. Her participation in events like the Cannes Film Festival demonstrates her commitment to promoting cinema's global nature and capacity to unite people from many backgrounds.

Monica's linguistic abilities extend beyond her professional life. As a mother, she is dedicated to teaching a love of language to her girls. She frequently tells stories about reading to them in many languages and urging them to embrace their multilingual ancestry. This dedication to education reflects her idea that language is an invaluable gift that can lead to new chances and experiences throughout life. She thinks introducing her children to various languages would inspire them to value the beauty of communication and the diversity of cultures.

Chapter 9

THE ART OF REINVENTION

Monica Bellucci's career is a beautiful example of the art of reinvention. She has expertly handled the entertainment industry's hurdles and upheavals from her early days as a model to prominence in international movies. What distinguishes her is her timeless beauty and her ability to adapt to the changing environment of film and fashion, seizing new chances while remaining committed to her artistic vision.

Monica's journey began in the 1990s when supermodels and a strong emphasis on glamor dominated the fashion business. She rapidly became a sensation, appearing on the covers of well-known magazines and walking runways for luxury labels. However, rather than being content with her modeling career, she recognized the transient nature of the fashion industry. Monica was determined to leave a more enduring impact and consciously pursued a career in acting, a move that took guts and flexibility. Her modeling experience, while valuable, needed to be improved to ensure success in film, where talent and versatility were vital.

Monica suffered skepticism and typecasting early in her acting career and was frequently judged based on her modeling background. However, she skillfully used her status to choose parts that pushed her and demonstrated her versatility. Her breakout part in *Malèna* (2000) was crucial in this sense; the film was not only about beauty but also about the complexity of feminine identity and desire. Through this play, she turned her image from a mere sex symbol to a severe actor capable of delivering powerful performances.

Monica evolved along with the film industry. The early 2000s saw substantial changes in cinematic storytelling, with an increased need for diverse narratives and nuanced characters. Recognizing this shift, Monica aggressively sought opportunities that challenged traditional assumptions. Her performances in films like

Irreversible (2002) and *The Passion of the Christ* (2004) were adventurous, demonstrating her willingness to take risks and push the envelope. In *Irreversible*, directed by Gaspar Noé, she played a character who had endured significant trauma, forcing audiences to confront hard facts about violence and vulnerability. This willingness to take on complicated and frequently contentious issues demonstrated her commitment to growing as an artist and remaining relevant in an industry progressively turning towards more progressive storytelling.

Monica's capacity to alter herself went beyond her choice of jobs. As the entertainment industry embraced the digital age, she recognized the significance of adapting to new platforms and viewers. In the face of shifting viewing preferences, she embraced social media to communicate with her supporters and give insights into her life and career. She humanized her celebrity position by building a presence on sites such as Instagram, allowing her fans to see the lady behind the dazzling façade. This method confirmed her relevance and allowed her to engage with a younger audience eager to connect with their idols on a more personal level.

Her work on high-profile movies like *Spectre* (2015) and *The Brothers Bloom* (2008) proved her adaptability and desire to engage with a wide range of filmmakers. Lucia Sciarra's work in the James Bond franchise was particularly noteworthy since it marked her entry into Hollywood while demonstrating her ability to play strong female characters. Despite being a Bond girl, Monica added depth to her part, depicting a lady of substance rather than a simple accessory to the male protagonist. This move was consistent with her larger objective to reinvent femininity in cinema, challenging the old clichés commonly associated with women in action films.

Monica is devoted to fostering emerging talent and participating in projects that reflect these ideals as the industry evolves. There is a greater emphasis on tales that feature varied voices and viewpoints. Her work with new filmmakers demonstrates her confidence in storytelling's ability to build cross-cultural connections and understanding. By promoting new voices, she not only helps the progress of the business but also strengthens her position as a mentor and advocate for change in the cinema community.

Monica's ability to remain relevant is also based on her honesty. She has frequently discussed the constraints placed on women in the entertainment industry around appearance and aging. Rather than giving in to these demands, Monica has embraced her uniqueness, arguing for a more extensive definition of beauty beyond age and conventional criteria. Her frank remarks about aging gracefully and celebrating one's journey have struck a chord with many, allowing her to retain a strong bond with her audience. She exemplifies that reinvention is more than external change; it also entails accepting oneself and maintaining security in one's talents.

Monica Bellucci is an excellent example of negotiating change with grace and sincerity in an age of rapid technological innovation and shifting cultural paradigms.

Her path through the complexity of the entertainment industry demonstrates the potential of reinvention—taking on new difficulties while remaining true to one's principles and purpose. In doing so, she has not only established a spectacular career for herself. Still, she has also encouraged numerous people to pursue their passions, reminding us that the art of reinvention is a never-ending journey full of possibilities.

Chapter 10

BEYOND THE SCREEN

Monica Bellucci's life is a tapestry woven with threads of beauty, talent, and unrelenting dedication to making a difference in the world. While she is known worldwide for her captivating performances and commanding presence on screen, her contributions extend far beyond the film business. Monica, a humanitarian, cultural ambassador, and fashion icon, has used her platform to inspire and uplift others around her, demonstrating that true influence is not based on celebrity but on the ability to effect positive change.

Monica has displayed a great sense of social duty since the beginning of her profession. She has been actively involved in various charity organizations, particularly on topics that align with her principles, such as women's rights, education, and health. One significant component of her philanthropic activity is her involvement as a spokesman for the Italian charity *Amici della Musica*, which promotes music instruction for poor youngsters. Monica believes in the transformational power of the arts, and her efforts to provide youngsters with access to music education demonstrate her passion for instilling creativity and self-expression in young minds. She has generated awareness and finances through her engagement, allowing children to explore their musical skills and find the joy of artistic expression.

Monica has also been an outspoken advocate for breast cancer awareness, sharing her personal experiences and encouraging people to prioritize their health. She recognizes the value of exposure in these talks and uses her public platform to bring attention to critical health concerns that are sometimes overlooked. By emphasizing the significance of frequent check-ups and early detection, she has inspired numerous women to make proactive efforts to manage their health, proving that true beauty is founded on self-care and awareness.

Monica's impact on fashion and culture is equally enormous. She personified elegance and sophistication as a model and actress, becoming a muse for several great designers, including Dolce & Gabbana. Her fashion work is more than just attractive; it demonstrates her understanding of artistry and admiration for the craftsmanship that goes into each piece. Monica's partnerships with designers accentuate her style while celebrating Italian fashion, establishing her as a cultural ambassador for her hometown. She has frequently been spotted in the front rows of fashion shows worldwide, perfectly merging high fashion with approachable style and pushing women to embrace their uniqueness.

Aside from her role as a style icon, Monica has continually challenged traditional notions of beauty and femininity. In a world where youth is frequently exalted, she has fearlessly spoken out against ageism and the excessive expectations placed on women in the profession. Monica pushes for a more inclusive definition of beauty that values authenticity, diversity, and the natural aging process. She believes that women should be encouraged to accept their individuality and that each stage of life has its beauty. Her message is powerful, pushing women to reframe their self-worth in terms of experiences and wisdom rather than conventional beauty standards.

Monica's cultural influence extends to her commitment to celebrating her Italian background while promoting a more profound understanding of global diversity. She frequently speaks warmly of her origins in Città di Castello and how her background influenced her views. Her work aims to transcend cultural divides by reminding audiences that cinema is a universal language capable of creating understanding and connection amongst disparate populations. By representing Italian cinema on international stages, she has helped to raise awareness of foreign films and the unique storylines they provide.

Monica has also played an essential role in developing the next generation of artists. As a well-known figure in the entertainment world, she serves as a role model for aspiring actors and models, demonstrating how patience and hard work can lead to success. Her path, filled with struggles and victories, emphasizes the significance of perseverance in the face of adversity. Monica inspires young women to follow their aspirations while remaining true to themselves and their values.

In addition to her artistic talents, Monica's humanitarian initiatives demonstrate her dedication to social justice. She has participated in gender equality initiatives and utilized her platform to advocate for the rights of women and marginalized populations. Her commitment to projects to eliminate violence against women demonstrates her knowledge of today's concerns and determination to make a difference.

Monica's influence extends beyond her on-screen performances and modeling career, permeating her life and work. She illustrates how celebrity status may be used for good, and she actively strives to inspire others to join her in this effort. Her many contributions to humanitarian work, fashion, and culture reflect a lady who is equally passionate about social issues as her profession.

Chapter 11

LEGACY OF AN ICON

Monica Bellucci is a towering personality in contemporary cinema, fashion, and popular culture, making an enduring impression on spectators and artists. Her legacy extends beyond her roles and fashion choices; it is woven into the fabric of contemporary arts and self-expression, representing her path as a versatile talent who has redefined views of beauty, femininity, and honesty.

Monica has made significant and diverse contributions to cinema. Her breakthrough performance in *Malèna* (2000) demonstrated her excellent acting abilities and ability to embody complicated emotions and tales. As the titular heroine, she handled issues of love, sorrow, and societal judgment, which struck a profound chord with viewers. Critics commended her for a realistic representation of a woman struggling with her identity in a patriarchal environment. This part catapulted her to international stardom, establishing her as a serious actress capable of giving tremendous performances. Monica continued to play challenging roles that defied traditional stereotypes, such as her portrayal of a strong female character in *The Passion of the Christ* (2004) and her mesmerizing presence in *Spectre* (2015), where she played the enigmatic Lucia Sciarra, reaffirming her status as a Bond girl with depth and complexity.

Monica's influence extends to the fashion industry, where she is long regarded as a style icon. Her collaborations with prominent designers, including Dolce & Gabbana, have had a long-lasting impact on the industry, sparking innumerable fashion trends and defining new beauty standards. She is well-known for her elegance and confidence, having adorned the covers of major fashion magazines and walked the runways of essential fashion events, where her unique ability to merge traditional splendor with contemporary chic has been universally acclaimed. Monica has redefined beauty, emphasizing that it may take numerous forms and that true elegance is based on sincerity and self-assurance.

Furthermore, Monica's impact on pop culture goes far beyond the silver screen and fashion runways. She has become a symbol of female empowerment, embodying strength, resilience, and the value of individuality. In interviews, she has frequently highlighted her thoughts on aging and beauty standards, calling for a more inclusive definition of femininity that includes all stages of life. Monica's honesty about her experiences has inspired many to embrace their individuality, defying traditional standards about how women should appear and act. Her approach to aging is refreshingly honest, urging people to find beauty in their experiences rather than submitting to artificial expectations.

Her work has also shaped Monica's legacy as an Italian cultural ambassador. She has elevated Italian cinema to the forefront of international acclaim, bridging cultural divides through storytelling. She has helped broaden global cinema understanding by working on projects that emphasize creativity while engaging with international directors. Her partnerships with directors from various backgrounds demonstrate her versatility and devotion to discovering rich, diverse themes that appeal to a broad audience.

Monica's influence is also reflected in her ability to connect with the younger generation. As social media continues to alter how celebrities interact with followers, Monica has expertly negotiated the landscape, using sites such as Instagram to reveal glimpses of her life and work while preserving a sense of mystery. Her postings frequently reflect her artistic interests and personal philosophy, encouraging her readers to value art, fashion, and cultural heritage. By embracing this new communication approach, she has remained relevant and relatable, allowing her legacy to flourish while remaining true to her beginnings.

Monica's humanitarian work adds another element to her legacy. Her dedication to various humanitarian causes, notably those promoting women's rights and education, illustrates her appreciation of using one's power for the greater good. This dedication improves her public image and establishes her as a leader in fighting for positive change. Her acts serve as a reminder that true effect is defined not by celebrity but by how one contributes to society and empowers others.

Monica Bellucci's legacy grows with time. She is more than just a famous actress or a fashion star; she symbolizes courage and honesty in an ever-changing world. Her ability to reinvent herself while remaining faithful to her roots inspires many, demonstrating that excellent craftsmanship has no borders. Monica's tale reflects the strength of resilience, beauty, and the lasting impact one may have on the world. Reflecting on her legacy, we recognize the value of embracing one's uniqueness, questioning conventional standards, and utilizing our voices to inspire others. Monica Bellucci will always be remembered as an icon whose influence lasts centuries.

CONCLUSION

Monica Bellucci's life and career unfold in a riveting story of passion, resilience, and artistry. From her humble origins in Città di Castello to her emergence as a global icon, her path exemplifies the rise of an excellent actress and the evolution of a woman who has constantly reinterpreted her role in a changing society. Each stage of her life reveals a steadfast dedication to her craft and a genuine acceptance of her identity.

Monica has gracefully handled the difficulties of celebrity and talent throughout her career, selecting roles that defy conventional expectations while expressing femininity's varied character. Her ability to portray profound emotions and embody varied roles has helped her leave an indelible mark on the film industry, encouraging innumerable aspiring actors and actresses. Her influence extends beyond the silver screen to fashion and society, where she has become a symbol of confidence, elegance, and empowerment. Her thoughts on beauty and aging resonate with women worldwide, inspiring them to embrace their genuine selves in a society that frequently imposes restrictive standards of merit.

Furthermore, Monica's bilingual abilities and eagerness to examine stories from various cultures demonstrate her confidence in the universality of human experience. She builds bridges between groups, encouraging a broader awareness of the diversity of world film. Her humanitarian initiatives and fight for women's rights compound her effect, reminding us that genuine legacy is more than personal accomplishments; it is also about inspiring positive change in others.

Monica Bellucci continues her artistic journey, embodying the idea that life is a constant reinvention rather than a stagnant existence. Her resilience in the face of adversity and her capacity to adapt to new trends and ideas guarantee that her tale is still relevant. Each new endeavor she embarks on adds another dimension to her legacy, inviting us to witness the unfolding of her story while challenging us to reflect on our own.

Monica exemplifies the power of honesty and self-expression in the ever-changing landscape of fame and craft. Her journey is far from over, and as she pursues new channels of creativity and influence, we are reminded that great icons transcend the confines of their fields. Monica Bellucci is more than just an actress or a model; she is a symbol of strength, a voice for change, and a reflection of the beauty of accepting one's uniqueness.

As we conclude this chapter in her life and work, we look forward to her timeless path, which inspires us all. Monica Bellucci's narrative reminds us that with passion, tenacity, and an unshakeable sense of self, we, too, can manage life's complications and leave our distinctive mark on the world. Her legacy shines as a beacon of hope, illuminating the route for future generations of artists and dreamers, inspiring them to go on their journeys of self-discovery and creative exploration.

www.ingramcontent.com/pod-product-compliance
Lightning Source LLC
Chambersburg PA
CBHW070359230526
45471CB00006B/2638